TOPIC

The One Who Made You Knows You

SCRIPTURES

1. **Psalm 139:1** — O Lord, You have searched me and known me.

2. **Romans 8:26,27** — Likewise the Spirit also helps in our weaknesses. For we do not know what we should pray for as we ought, but the Spirit Himself makes intercession.... Now He who searches the hearts knows what the mind of the Spirit is, because He makes intercession for the saints according to the will of God.

3. **1 Corinthians 2:9,10** — But as it is written: "Eye has not seen, nor ear heard, nor have entered into the heart of man the things which God has prepared for those who love Him. But God has revealed them to us through His Spirit. For the Spirit searches all things, yes the deep things of God.

SYNOPSIS

The four lessons in this study, *How Good Is God?*, will focus on the following topics:

- The One Who Made You Knows You

- The Overwhelming Love of God

- Darkness Will Never Overcome the Light of God in You!

- God Has A Wonderful Book About You

One of the most important things we need to remember as believers might seem basic, but it is absolutely crucial to our relationship with God: we need to remember that God is good, and He loves us. Our view of God's character is truly a game-changing factor that affects our faith, our thinking, and our choices in countless ways. It's so important that what we think about God is true, especially in how He loves us and relates to us as His children.

The emphasis of this lesson:

God searches your heart through the presence of His Holy Spirit. He loves you so much, and He is always present with you and attentive to you as you go about your everyday life. In every moment of your life, He wants to be there for you, comfort you, teach you, and provide everything you need. When we choose to embrace His correction and wisdom, we come closer to Him and escape temptation.

God Searches and Knows You Through His Holy Spirit

In Psalm 139, we see a stunning picture of God's love for us in one of King David's conversations with Him. His psalm begins: "O Lord, You have searched me and known me" (Psalm 139:1).

You might be wondering; *How does God search me and know me?* His Holy Spirit is living in you, and the first thing you need to know about Him is that He'll never leave you or abandon you. He is the best Friend you will ever have. He is always with you, no matter what you're going through or how long it's been since you felt like you were worthy enough to talk to Him.

The Holy Spirit didn't decide to come into your heart as if you were a hotel or an apartment; He's not paying a price to live there for just a few days, a month, a year, or even two years. Jesus paid the price for all of you — forever. Then He came in to dwell in you as His house through His Holy Spirit. He loves you so much that He wants to be with you every minute, every second of every day. Yes, the Holy Spirit is *that* good and *that* wonderful!

The Holy Spirit Has ALL Knowledge

The second thing you need to know about the Holy Spirit is that He's absolutely brilliant. He knows everything — all knowledge for all time is in His power to give. Whenever and wherever you need to know something, He has the answer you're looking for.

The Bible says if we draw near to God, He will draw near to us (*see* James 4:8), which is also something He does through His Holy Spirit. Have you ever experienced the power of the Holy Spirit to touch and change your heart, and to open your eyes to something that you can't see normally?

A Note From Denise Renner

The Word of God is so powerful in our lives. It is essential that every person spend time with God and study His Word in order to stay spiritually strong in these last days.

This study guide corresponds to my *TIME With Denise Renner* TV program by the same title that can be viewed at **deniserenner.org**. My desire is that through these lessons, you find the encouragement and freedom in Christ that you need. I believe the Holy Spirit is going to speak to you through the words you read in this study tool and that as you begin to use it, you will be *propelled* into the abundant life God has planned for you. I encourage you to make the effort to receive all He has for you and all He wants to do in you — it will definitely be worth it!

Whether you have walked with the Lord a long time or have just begun to follow Him, there is so much He wants to give you from His Word. He sees where you are, and He wants to meet you there.

> Therefore do not worry about tomorrow, for tomorrow
> will worry about its own things.
> Sufficient for the day is its own trouble.
> — Matthew 6:34

Your sister and friend in Jesus Christ,

Denise Renner

Denise Renner

How Good Is God?

Published by Rick Renner Ministries
www.renner.org

ISBN 13: 978-1-6675-1100-9

ISBN 13 eBook: 978-1-6675-1101-6

Denise shared about a time when the Holy Spirit did that for her. Once when she was tempted to judge someone, the Holy Spirit showed her one of that person's good qualities and how this individual had no idea of the mistake she was making. His patient reminder helped Denise forgive her and appreciate the positive things she did for her.

This isn't our natural response to someone frustrating us, but it is the supernatural evidence that the Holy Spirit — who knows all things — is revealing truth to us about a situation. That brings us to the third thing that's so amazing about the Holy Spirit: He has an amazing reputation and ability to guide us into truth and away from the lies that hurt us.

That's the power of the Holy Spirit, and He's in you when you're born again. The Bible also says that when you're baptized in the Holy Spirit, He's the One who fills you with power. How amazing is that?

The Holy Spirit Is Our Comforter

When Jesus gave us the Holy Spirit, He wasn't trying to withhold something about Himself from us. He was trying to get something — everything — about Himself *to* us. And the Holy Spirit includes the whole person of Jesus, so when He's speaking to us, it's as if we were talking directly to Jesus.

The fourth aspect of the Holy Spirit that is such a life-changing gift is His ability to comfort us. His comforting power is absolutely beyond any loving spouse, friend, food, drug, entertainment, or possession we can find on this earth. Even when those things do bring a level of comfort, *His* comfort is so much better.

Even when we feel like what we're going through is totally unbearable, the situation seems only to be getting worse, and we start to feel as if we're in a deep, dark hole, the Holy Spirit is *right there*. He gets into that hole with us, and like a supernatural elevator, He comes alongside and underneath us, and He steadily works to raise us up to a place where our thinking is normal and healthy, we have peace in our heart, and strength in our body. His attribute of comfort is such a tremendous gift.

The Holy Spirit Is the Best Teacher

The fifth aspect of the Holy Spirit we need to know is that He is a great teacher. Do you remember your favorite teachers from school? The best teachers were usually incredibly encouraging; they never put down their students. The Holy Spirit is that way. He is always right, but He's never harsh or rude; He states the truth, but He will never put you down.

At times we may have had people in a superior position over us — like parents, teachers, bosses, older siblings, or even a spouse — who tried to teach us something, but because they weren't the perfect teacher like the Holy Spirit, they ended up deeply hurting us in the process. Maybe they put us down, maybe they were rude, or maybe they were harsh; whatever the case, when imperfect humans tried to teach us something with imperfect teaching methods, there may be bruises along the way. But the good news is that the Holy Spirit is a perfect teacher, and there will never be any bruises or wounds from Him as He teaches you.

The Holy Spirit Is Our Greatest Friend

The Holy Spirit is truly the greatest friend you will ever have; He is the One who is always with you, never leaves your side, and never wants to be away from you, not even for a second. He loves you so much that He came to live inside of you as your Teacher, your Comforter, and your Guide. He's also a great searcher. Again, Psalm 139:1 says, "O Lord, You have *searched* me and known me."

The Holy Spirit loves you so much that He's always searching your heart; He knows you from the inside out. Likewise, Rick Renner, Denise's husband, really loves history, and he has a passion for bringing history and the Bible together for people. He's always watching the History Channel on television and buying books that teach him the history of Italy, Egypt, Greece, and other places because he genuinely loves history. His love for the subject makes him more than willing to invest time, effort, and finances to learn more about it.

In the same manner, Denise was trained as an opera singer and absolutely loves the study of the human voice and what the voice can do. Whether it's opera, pop, or rock, she's interested in many genres of music because they all showcase the voice and display how the body works with the voice. Sometimes she'll watch a program where they have many talented singers because she loves listening to the wide range of voices and discovering more about what the voice can do.

He Wants To Bring the Answers and Solutions You Need

Similarly, the Holy Spirit loves *you* so much — you are His favorite subject! That's one reason why He's always searching your spirit — to reveal to you how much He loves you. It's like He's always asking, "How can I reveal more truth to her?" or "How can I provide comfort for her?" Isn't He wonderful? Romans 8:26 tells us more about His searching power. It says,

> **Likewise the Spirit also helps in our weaknesses. For we do not know what we should pray for as we ought, but the Spirit Himself makes intercession….**

Do you see that? The Holy Spirit knows our weaknesses, but He doesn't run from them. Instead, He helps us in the middle of our weaknesses. So often we don't know how to pray the way we need to pray because life, feelings, and so many other factors cloud our ability to see clearly. But the Holy Spirit lives inside each of us, and He begins to make intercession, or pray for us with groanings and words which cannot be uttered. Continuing with verse 27, we learn:

> **Now He who searches the hearts knows what the mind of the Spirit is, because He makes intercession for the saints according to the will of God.**

As the Holy Spirit searches your heart, He reveals what you need and makes intercession for you. When you are down, He's saying, "Don't give up — you can do all things through Me!" When you're disappointed, He's saying, "It's okay. Cry out to Me, and I will help you. I'm the Encourager, and I live in you." When someone tries to trick you with lies and deceit, the Holy Spirit says, "No, no, no, that's not the truth. You know the truth — you know what I've been teaching you. Stand for the truth."

That's the power, love, and commitment of the Holy Spirit; He will be there for you even in your weaknesses. He will never leave you — no matter how many times you fall. Thank God He will never run from you or condemn you. Instead, He will always be right by your side to help you.

Every time you find yourself feeling weak, you can pray a very powerful prayer: *Holy Spirit, help. Help me with this problem. Help me give my heart to these people. Help me to continue and not quit. Help me be strong when my body wants to be weak.*

You can ask the Holy Spirit to help you because He's made an investigative search of your heart and knows the specific help you need. That's how much He loves you!

The Holy Spirit Has Wisdom For Every Situation

Let's take a look at First Corinthians 2:9 and 10 for more insight about the Holy Spirit.

> **But as it is written: "Eye has not seen, nor ear heard, nor have entered into the heart of man the things which God has prepared for those who love Him." But God has revealed them to us through His Spirit. For the Spirit searches all things, yes the deep things of God.**

The Holy Spirit is searching you because He ultimately wants to reveal to you the deepest truths of God. On the program, Denise shared how the Holy Spirit had searched her heart and revealed a truth she needed to know. Years ago, Denise had found fault in a particular person and thought that person just needed to change, but the Holy Spirit wanted to show Denise something else. Denise didn't realize she had unforgiveness in her heart until the Holy Spirit gently said, "No, Denise, you need to take responsibility for *your* heart, and you need to forgive. You have unforgiveness and bitterness in your heart, and they are destroying your life and your health. You need to forgive. You need to set that person free."

When the Holy Spirit revealed to Denise that she had unforgiveness and bitterness in her heart and needed to forgive this person, Denise chose forgiveness. And when she did, she was set free from two years of pain and torment, and confusion about *why* she was in pain. She'd been dealing with anxiety and severely cold hands and feet — even her face was hurting. But the moment she forgave that person and released her from her prison of guilt, Denise was free to receive all that God had for *her*, which included healing for her body.

And what He did for Denise, He wants to do for you. If you have sickness in your body, He's not trying to keep you in that sickness to teach you something — that's why Jesus went to the Cross: to pay the price for your healing. That's how much He loves you. When you have pain or sickness in your body, He wants to get the solution to you. In fact, He wants you to have that answer more than you do. The moment sickness and disease try to attack our body, the Holy Spirit is searching and asking, "How can I get the answer to them?"

You might be asking, "Well, doesn't the Holy Spirit also reveal my sin?" Yes, He does, but He doesn't reveal sin to you to condemn you. Jesus already took all the punishment and all the condemnation for sin, so you and I are completely forgiven. He comes with His Spirit to convict you and bring you to a place of repentance — *not* to make you feel guilty.

What's the difference between condemnation and conviction? Well, condemnation usually sounds something like this: "Oh, you're awful. You're terrible. You're a bad Christian. You disappointed God. You deserve whatever pain you have. You have unbelief in your heart. Don't you remember how you spoke to that person yesterday?" That's the voice of condemnation, which expresses very strong disapproval, and it comes from the enemy of your soul.

In contrast, the Holy Spirit uses conviction to speak to you gently. He may say things like, "This part of your life is not right, but I'm going to show you how to get out of it." He will encourage you and lead you to the Word of God and His great and precious promises that are within it (*see* 2 Peter 1:4).

The Holy Spirit makes a way of escape through conviction. His conviction brings you to the point where you say, "I agree with You, God. Please help me get out of this," and He, your Comforter and Guide, shows you the way out.

God truly does love you more than you can imagine. He never wants us to wonder if He doesn't love us or if what He gives to us will hurt us. James 1:17 is a wonderful reminder. It says, "Every good gift and every perfect gift is from above, and comes down from the Father of lights, with whom there is no variation or shadow of turning." What He has for us is always good — always.

What the devil tries to give us is bad. Whether it's physical illness, mental and emotional illness, financial lack, or other forms of attack, his goal is always to steal, kill, and destroy. But God doesn't give us bad things — *He gives us good things* — and He wants us to experience a vibrant and full life (*see* John 10:10). He's put the Holy Spirit inside us to search our heart daily, reveal to us how good He is, and prove His perfect, unconditional love for us.

STUDY QUESTIONS

Study to shew thyself approved unto God, a workman that
needeth not to be ashamed, rightly dividing the word of truth.
— 2 Timothy 2:15

1. The Holy Spirit is often misunderstood by believers because many people have misrepresented who He is, what He's about, and what it looks like to be led by Him. What are a few characteristics of the Holy Spirit that we can count on as we draw close to Him (*see* Romans 8:26 and 15:13; Isaiah 11:2; John 14:26 and 16:13; and James 4:5)?

2. Have you ever thought that God was trying to "teach you a lesson" through sickness, financial challenge, or another kind of difficult life circumstance? What do you think about the situation now in light of what you've learned? What stands out to you about this in Job 1 and James 1:17?

PRACTICAL APPLICATION

But be ye doers of the word, and not hearers only,
deceiving your own selves.
—James 1:22

1. In the same way that God searched David, He searches our hearts today through His Holy Spirit. What is one area of life that has seemed confusing to you lately? Where do you need His help, clarity, and direction? Invite Him to make your path clear and listen for His guiding voice. (*See* Proverbs 3:5,6 and Isaiah 30:21.)

2. The Holy Spirit is not only your Searcher, but He is also your Teacher, your Comforter, and your closest Friend — the One who promised to NEVER leave you or forsake you. Have you ever thought of Him as your Friend? Next time you feel lonely, ask Him to show you what it means to have Him as your best Friend and lean into His presence.

TOPIC

The Overwhelming Love of God

SCRIPTURES

1. **Psalm 139:1-10** — O Lord, You have searched me and known me. You know my sitting down and my rising up; you understand my thought afar off. You comprehend my path and my lying down, and are acquainted with all my ways. For there is not a word on my tongue, but behold, O Lord, You know it altogether. You have hedged me behind and before, and laid Your hand upon me. Such knowledge is too wonderful for me; it is high, I cannot attain it. Where can I go from Your Spirit? Or where can I flee from Your presence? If I ascend into heaven, You are there; If I make my bed in hell, behold, You are there. If I take the wings of the morning, and dwell in the uttermost parts of the sea, even there Your hand shall lead me, and Your right hand shall hold me.

2. **Hebrews 2:18** — For in that He Himself has suffered, being tempted, He is able to aid those who are tempted.

3. **Isaiah 41:10,13** — Fear not, for I am with you; be not dismayed, for I am your God. I will strengthen you, Yes, I will help you, and I will uphold you with My righteous right hand.... For I, the Lord your God, will hold your right hand, saying to you, "Fear not, I will help you."

SYNOPSIS

It is truly incredible how intimately God knows and loves you — every single birthmark, quirk, and tendency — and He's keenly aware of your every need. His heart towards you is GOOD, and He wants only the best for you. He has provided a way of escape from every temptation you may face and has equipped you to help you through every situation you will encounter. No matter how far you may run from Him or how many mistakes you have made or will make, He will always be right there waiting for you to draw near to Him.

The emphasis of this lesson:

God has full, intimate knowledge of your every need, hope, hurt, and challenge, and wants to see you not just survive, but *thrive*. When you lean into His Spirit, He'll help you avoid temptation, get back up when you stumble, and receive His unceasing and unconditional love for you.

In Lesson 1, we learned about how good God is, and how when we're born again, He puts the Holy Spirit, the Great Comforter, Teacher, Guide, and Searcher of our heart inside us to stay with us forever. He will never abandon us. Isn't it miraculous how much He loves us and wants to be involved in every aspect of our lives?

It's so exciting to study Psalm 139 because it shows so intimately how much God loves us, how His attention is on us, and how we can't ever escape His love because it's an eternal fact. We've already studied the first verse, which says, "O Lord, You have searched me and known me."

One of the things we learned about the Holy Spirit is how He's always searching inside you; He's searching to learn more about you and how to help you in your weakness. He convicts us of sin, He comforts us, and He reassures us it's going to be okay even when a challenge or pain feels almost unbearable. That's the power of the Holy Spirit's loving voice.

God's Heart Towards You Is GOOD

It's so very important that we're able to receive His love and encouragement because we all will be confronted with hard times at some point in life. And when they come, we *really* need to know what we believe, or we'll drift away from the truth of Scripture and become uncertain about God's heart towards us in the middle of the pain.

Oftentimes the enemy will lie to us and send us thoughts like, *Oh, well… this sickness is here because God's trying to teach me something*, or *I'm going through bankruptcy because God's trying to teach me to be patient.*

Friend, let me tell you this truth: God does not need disease, bankruptcy, or anything else the enemy might try to send into your life to teach you *anything*. He has the Holy Spirit inside you as your Teacher, and He doesn't need or use any of the devil's tactics to teach you. That's why we need to know God's true character; God is good — even when something bad happens. We need to have the right outlook. One that says, *I don't understand why this is happening, but I know that my God is good, He loves me, and He's working things out for my benefit.*

Psalm 139:2 says,

> **You know my sitting down and my rising up….**

Who cares about when you sit down or rise up? God does! It's amazing that God knew when you would sit down to read this, and He knows when you will get up from where you're sitting. He knows! He knows when you're going to lay down tonight and when you'll get up tomorrow morning. There are more than seven billion people in the world, and He knows when *every single one* of them sits in a chair, lays down, or stands up. What attention to detail our God has to each of our lives!

You may ask, "Is this really true?" Is David having a revelation of the goodness of God that's so hard for our minds to understand? It *is* difficult to understand, but it is necessary to believe. It's vital to our relationship with God that we *believe* His Word concerning how close He is to us and how aware He is of every thought we have and every move we make.

He Understands Every Single Detail About You

Psalm 139:2 continues, "You know my sitting down and my rising up; You *understand* my thought afar off." The Hebrew word for "understand" denotes *to sift* or *to scrutinize*. God scrutinizes the thoughts that are still being conceptualized in your head. Even when you're still processing information or not truly sure what you think about something, He knows that thought before you even think it, and He knows your words even before you speak them.

David's psalm continues in verse 3. He said,

> **You comprehend my path and my lying down, and are acquainted with all my ways.**

God knows all about you — *all* your works, *all* your words, *all* your ways, and even all your thoughts while they're still forming. And this knowledge is so huge, that it even includes your tendencies. He knows if you're a fan of coffee or if you don't enjoy the outdoors. He knows if you feel more at home on a hike or in an art museum and even the types of music, books, and stories that capture your heart. He knows and is attentive to all the details of your likes, dislikes, preferences, and tendencies. Are these things earth-shattering? No, but these are the intimate details about you that your God knows. He knows because He loves you, and He cares about every detail of your life.

Think about it: God loves you so much that He left Heaven in all its glory, took on the form of a human being, and subjected Himself to being denied, accused, and misunderstood over and over again. Then He voluntarily submitted himself to utter humiliation and a beating that tore His flesh from His body before He went to the Cross to lay down His life for you. He didn't take all that punishment as God; He had set aside His divinity — His God-ship — to endure all these things as a man who was seeking after God. He did that for *you*, and He did all that for me because He loves us.

Jesus Walked Through Every Single Challenge You Have

The Bible says in Hebrews 4:15 that Jesus was tempted in every single way that we've ever been or ever will be tempted. He never sinned, but He was tempted in every possible way so He could understand our struggles and have mercy on us. The incredible, intimate love that He has for us even extends to showing us grace for our most vulnerable weaknesses. Hebrews 2:18 declares:

> **For in that He Himself has suffered, being tempted, He is able to aid those who are tempted.**

He was tempted so He could help us when *we* are tempted. He laid down glory, took on human flesh, and experienced human pain, rejection, denial, false accusations, and suffering beyond what we could understand so He could help us when we are tempted — this is amazing, sacrificial *love*.

Our understanding of God's love needs to go deeper than simply saying, "Oh, yes. I know Jesus died for me." It needs to be so much fuller and deeper than that; the depth of His love should change our view of ourselves and others and how we interact with them. It should affect what we believe about our future and how we get up in the morning. God doesn't show us His love just so we can remain the same. He shows us His love and gives us the Holy Spirit so we can change and become more and more like Him.

God Gives Us Boundaries To Protect Us

Returning to Psalm 139, David said:

For there is not a word on my tongue, but behold, O Lord, You know it altogether. You have hedged me behind and before, and laid Your hand upon me.

— Psalm 139:4,5

David also let us know that our Lord has placed borders or boundaries around our life, which is actually an amazing gift. You are His, and He loves you so much that He surrounds you with a hedge of His protection. Like a good shepherd, He says, "Okay, I'm going to let go. I know you're not always thinking or doing right yet, but I'll let you go this far. I'll always know where you are and what you are thinking because I've placed a border around you to protect you."

You can't escape God's love. He does have boundaries for you because you're His child, and it's a good thing. You can't get away from Him; He loves you so much, and He will never leave you. Even if we start acting like stubborn sheep and start going off this way or that way, He has placed a hedge of protection around us to protect us from straying too far away. He will draw us back to where we can hear His voice and fellowship with Him.

Never forget that God's hand is on you and holding you, and His Spirit is always in you. He says in Isaiah 41:10 and 13:

Fear not, for I am with you; be not dismayed, for I am your God. I will strengthen you, Yes, I will help you, and I will uphold you with My righteous right hand....For I, the Lord your God, will hold your right hand, saying to you, 'Fear not, I will help you.'

His hand is always there to guide, comfort, and help you. You're never alone because the Holy Spirit is inside you, and He's hedged you in, behind and before, to protect you — that is the love of God.

When parents don't give their children any borders or boundaries, chaos ensues. Denise shared a story about a parent who told their babysitter that they never tell their children "no" because they didn't want to quench the children's creativity. Even if the house was destroyed in the process, the parents wouldn't stop them. Sadly, the lack of boundaries and discipline was effectively abandoning their children.

When parents say to their children, "You can do whatever you want," through their words and actions, they set up their children to be overwhelmed with the responsibility of creating their own boundaries. Consequently, the children do not feel safe or secure, and they end up acting out. It's an expression of love to establish borders with your children, and it's the love of our God that does the same for us.

He Will Never Leave You Nor Forsake You

David continued his description of God's overwhelming love in Psalm 139:6. He said:

> **Such knowledge is too wonderful for me; it is high, I cannot attain it.**

David confessed that God's love was beyond his ability to truly comprehend. In essence, David expressed, "How can it really be that God, the Maker of Heaven and Earth, loves me so much that He cares when I sit down or stand up, or about every single word in my mouth, and knows all my thoughts before I even think them? It's beyond me!"

Although God's infinite love may have been beyond David's ability to fully understand, he still believed and received all of God's love for him. In his Psalm, David asked God a question:

> **Where can I go from Your Spirit? Or where can I flee from Your presence?**
>
> **— Psalm 139:7**

Here the word "presence" in the Hebrew language denotes *the presence of the Trinity: God the Father, God the Son, and God the Holy Spirit*. David was saying that as a believer — as a child of God — you cannot escape the presence of the Father, you cannot escape His love, you cannot escape the power and the sacrifice that Jesus gave you through the Cross, and you cannot escape the loving presence of the Holy Spirit in you. And if you've been baptized in the Holy Spirit, you are filled with His power — you can't escape that.

As David continued his love song to his Heavenly Father, he attempted to answer his own question. Psalm 139:8-10 says:

> **If I ascend into heaven, you are there; If I make my bed in hell, behold, You are there. If I take the wings of the morning, and**

dwell in the uttermost parts of the sea, even there Your hand shall lead me, and Your right hand shall hold me.

Although he may have felt unable to fully comprehend God's love, David knew there was no escaping it, and he was comforted by that. No matter what you do or where you go, you can never escape the love of the Father, the tremendous sacrificial love of Jesus, His redeeming grace and mercy, or the presence of the powerful Holy Spirit. He will *never* leave you.

Do you have tears in your eyes right now? Maybe you're thinking, *I didn't know He loved me so much, and that there was still hope for me. I thought I did so much wrong. I'm a believer but I've done so much wrong. I thought He wouldn't receive me anymore, I thought I'd gone too far.* Guess what, dear friend? You have NOT gone too far. He's hedged you in behind and before, and His hand of blessing and protection is on you. It's not an accident that you're going through this series — He is ordering your steps (*see* Psalm 37:23).

The Holy Spirit is talking to you. He is gently wooing you back to Himself. He's saying, "You can't avoid My love any longer. You can't escape My presence. You are Mine. You're not your own, you're Mine. I treasure you."

STUDY QUESTIONS

Study to shew thyself approved unto God, a workman that needeth not to be ashamed, rightly dividing the word of truth.
— 2 Timothy 2:15

1. God's heart toward you is good — even when you go through difficult things, He is willing and able to bring beauty and redemption out of your pain. How did the Lord restore Job after all the troubles he went through? How does Job's story give you hope? (*See* Job 42:7-17.)

2. In Psalm 139:5, David declared that God has "hedged [us] behind and before." What did that promise look like in Jonah's life (*see* Jonah 1 and 2)? How does it comfort you to know that even when you run from God, He still remains with you and provides boundaries to keep you safe?

PRACTICAL APPLICATION

**But be ye doers of the word, and not hearers only,
deceiving your own selves.
—James 1:22**

1. How does it affect you to know that God is intimately aware of every
   detail about you — even the smallest, most seemingly insignificant
   things? What is one detail about you that comes to mind that brings
   you joy? Whether it's sipping your morning coffee, taking a walk, or
   spending time on a hobby you love, invite Him to enjoy it with you
   this week, and savor every moment with Him.

2. Scripture says that Jesus deeply understands the pain you've gone
   through and can identify with all the ways you've been tempted (*see*
   Hebrews 4:15,16). What wound or temptation seems to lurk around
   your life consistently? Thank Him that He understands and sympa-
   thizes with you, and ask Him to give you the specific strength you
   need to stand against the enemy's attacks and the endurance to keep
   going.

LESSON 3

TOPIC

Darkness Will Never Overcome the Light of God in You!

SCRIPTURES

1. **Psalm 139:6,7,10-12** — Such knowledge is too wonderful for me; it
   is high, I cannot attain it. Where can I go from Your Spirit? Or where
   can I flee from Your presence?...Even there Your hand shall lead
   me, and Your right hand shall hold me. If I say, "Surely the darkness
   shall fall on me," even the night shall be light about me; indeed, the
   darkness shall not hide from You, but the night shines as the day; the
   darkness and the light are both alike to You.

2. **Isaiah 41:10,13** — Fear not, for I am with you; be not dismayed, for I
   am your God. I will strengthen you, yes, I will help you; I will uphold

you with My righteous right hand...For I, the Lord your God, will hold your right hand, saying to you, "Fear not, I will help you."

3. **John 18:33-37** — Then Pilate entered the Praetorian again, called Jesus, and said to Him, "Are You the King of the Jews?" Jesus answered him, "Are you speaking for yourself about this, or did others tell you this concerning Me?" Pilate answered, "Am I a Jew? Your own nation and the chief priests have delivered You to me. What have You done?" Jesus answered, "My kingdom is not of this world. If My kingdom were of this world, My servants would fight, so that I should not be delivered to the Jews; but now My kingdom is not from here." Pilate therefore said to Him, "Are You a king then?" Jesus answered, "You say rightly that I am a king. For this cause I was born and for this cause I have come into the world, that I should bear witness to the truth. Everyone who is of the truth hears My voice."

4. **John 1:4-9** — In Him was life, and the life was the light of men. And the light shines in the darkness, and the darkness did not comprehend it. There was a man sent from God, whose name was John. This man came for a witness, to bear witness of the Light that all through him might believe. He was not that Light, but was sent to bear witness of that Light. That was the true Light which gives light to every man coming into the world.

5. **Revelation 21:23** — The city had no need of the sun or of the moon to shine in it, for the glory of God illuminated it. The Lamb is its light.

6. **Revelation 22:5** — There shall be no night there: They need no lamp nor light of the sun, for the Lord God gives them light. And they shall reign forever and ever.

SYNOPSIS

As we study Psalm 139, one of the most beautiful things we're realizing is the closeness and sweetness of God's love for us. His love is so intimate, vast, and overwhelming, which is what David was trying to communicate in this psalm to the Lord.

The emphasis of this lesson:

God's love for you is so great that it's impossible to fully understand this side of Heaven. No matter where you go, He is right there *with* you and *for* you in every struggle. The light of His Spirit in you chases away and

displaces all the darkness that was once inside you and gives you new life.

God's Love Is Greater Than We Can Comprehend

It is not known for certain when David wrote Psalm 139, but with his life experiences, we know he had an abundance of opportunities to discover God's character and love for him. After decades of abiding with God, worshiping Him, and experiencing His protection in the middle of countless dangers and dilemmas, David had come out of battle after battle victorious. His grasp of the Father's love for him was firsthand, yet he was still awestruck. In Psalm 139:6, David wrote:

> **Such knowledge is too wonderful for me; it is high, I cannot attain it.**

It's as if David was saying, "God, Your love is so big and so infinite that I can't fully understand it." In the same way, we can certainly relate to David — we may not fully understand the greatness of God's love, but we can *believe it* and *receive it*. Then in verse 7, David asked:

> **Where can I go from Your Spirit? Or where can I flee from Your presence?**

The word "presence" here is a translation from a Hebrew word that means *faces*. Many scholars have determined that David was saying, "I can't flee from *the Trinity — the faces of the Father, the Son*, and *the Holy Spirit*." David didn't have the Holy Spirit *in* him the way we do today, but he had *experiences* with the Holy Spirit and things that were revealed to him *by* the Holy Spirit.

David had an understanding of redemption, of a mighty God that would empower him against his enemy, and of the constant presence of the Spirit of God who would never leave or forsake His children. When talking about Heaven, hell, the earth, and even the most remote, vast places of land and sea, David said,

> **Even there Your hand shall lead me, and Your right hand shall hold me.**
>
> **— Psalm 139:10**

His Presence Chases Away the Darkness

If you are born again, a believer in Jesus Christ, the hand of God is on you and will never leave you. In the same vein, we can see this clearly in Isaiah 41:10 and 13:

> **Fear not, for I am with you; be not dismayed, for I am your God. I will strengthen you, yes, I will help you; I will uphold you with My righteous right hand....For I, the Lord your God, will hold your right hand, saying to you, "Fear not, I will help you."**

Take a moment and just imagine it: Imagine that God is holding you by your right hand, saying "Don't be afraid, son. Don't be afraid, daughter. I'm with you, and I will help you." If you're in a rough situation right now, just know in your heart that God is holding you by His hand and saying those very words to you.

We can take comfort in this precious promise because it's true. God's Word is truth, and it's there to teach, comfort, and encourage us in our everyday life (*see* 2 Timothy 3:16,17). The Bible says that Heaven and earth will pass away, but *His Word* will never pass away (*see* Matthew 24:35). And that same solid, unchanging Word says that He's holding you by the hand and promising you that He'll give you the strength to face whatever comes. What a gift!

Furthermore, Psalm 139:11 says,

> **If I say, "Surely the darkness shall fall on me," even the night shall be light about me.**

The Word of God testifies to the fact that your confession is critically important. What you say out of your mouth about yourself and your situation needs to agree with the truth because there's power in not just your confession but *believing* your confession. David knew that even if dark and uncertain times were to confront him, he would have nothing to fear because God — the Light and Truth — would surround him.

Jesus Used His Words On Purpose To Further His Destiny

Jesus was the premier example of having a good confession in the middle of difficult circumstances (*see* 1 Timothy 6:13). As He stood before Pilate, enormous pressure hung over Jesus; the Jews had already mistreated, accused, and arrested Him; Peter had already denied Him; Judas had already betrayed Him; and the other disciples had already left Him. Yet, in the midst of this betrayal, He didn't relinquish the power of His words to the enemy. He held to the truth of who He was in His confession and used His words intentionally to further the Father's plan, even when Satan was fighting hard to get Him to do the opposite.

And the enemy tries to do the same to us. He speaks his lies and applies unbelievable pressure on us, trying to get us to let go of our confession of faith. The enemy will try to fill our minds with thoughts like these:

You don't believe that — you know you can't really be healed.

You don't really believe that you can have peace in your marriage.

God can't actually bless you.

You know you can't be free of that temptation.

That relationship is beyond hope.

Not even God can deliver your child from addiction.

Remember when your friend prayed for the same thing? It didn't happen for them — why in the world do you think it would happen for you?

When the enemy comes with his pressure, doubt, and confusion, remember that he used the same tactics on Jesus too. The Bible says Jesus was tempted in every way that we are tempted (*see* Hebrews 4:14-16). Standing before an angry crowd with the Roman governor of Judea, Jesus was under greater pressure than ever before, yet He wasn't moved.

> **Then Pilate entered the Praetorian again, called Jesus, and said to Him, "Are You the King of the Jews?"**
>
> **Jesus answered him, "Are you speaking for yourself about this, or did others tell you this concerning Me?"**
>
> **Pilate answered, "Am I a Jew? Your own nation and the chief priests have delivered You to me. What have You done?"**
>
> **Jesus answered, "My kingdom is not of this world. If My kingdom were of this world, My servants would fight, so that I**

should not be delivered to the Jews; but now My kingdom is not from here."

Pilate therefore said to Him, "Are You a king then?"

Jesus answered, "You say rightly that I am a king. For this cause I was born and for this cause I have come into the world, that I should bear witness to the truth. Everyone who is of the truth hears My voice."

—John 18:33-37

Jesus never backed down from His confession of who He was or what He was sent to do — even when He was faced with certain death. He spoke the truth of God's Word over Himself and His situation. And with His help — with His power and strength — we can boldly declare God's Word over our situation too. He is the strength we need for every situation and the Light that makes our way clear. Meditate on this encouraging word from John 1:4-9.

In Him was life, and the life [Jesus] was the light of men. And the light shines in the darkness, and the darkness did not comprehend it. There was a man sent from God, whose name was John [the Baptist]. This man came for a witness, to bear witness of the Light, that all through him might believe. He was not that Light but was sent to bear witness of that Light. That was the true Light which gives light to every man coming into the world.

God Isn't Just THE Light, He is YOUR Light

God was mindful and loving to show Himself real to David in a way that he could understand — He was a lamp to David's feet and a light to his path (*see* Psalm 119:105). David wrote those words as a reminder of God's faithfulness to guide and direct him — and that reminder is just as important to us today. Even when we don't say the right thing, God is so merciful that even then, He still lights up the darkness. That's His unconditional, undeserved love coming to us in the person of Jesus, who is inside us through the presence of the Holy Spirit until we meet Him in eternity.

There's another verse in the Bible that says Jesus is our light, and that He will still be our light in Heaven. Revelation 21:23 declares,

The city had no need of the sun or of the moon to shine in it, for the glory of God illuminated it. *The Lamb is its light.*

When Jesus rose from the dead, His *light* did not dim — it just filled the halls of Heaven when He ascended! Angels worship Him constantly and are in awe of the way He laid down His life to redeem mankind. And a deposit of that Light has been placed inside you through the Person of the Holy Spirit. Revelation 22:5 proclaims,

There shall be no night there: They need no lamp nor light of the sun, for the Lord God gives them light. And they shall reign forever and ever.

That's our future — with Him in eternity! Can you imagine what it will be like to have no more night, ever? Can you imagine what it will be like to be immersed in the light of Christ, forever and ever? In Him — and in His Spirit in you — there is not even a hint of darkness. Your spirit is completely perfect; it looks just like Jesus — total light.

This is what the Holy Spirit did when He came to live in you: He extinguished and displaced the darkness that was in you. When we believe by faith that Jesus is Lord and that He was raised from the dead, His Spirit comes in and overwhelms the darkness with His light, filling the inside of us with complete light — because *in Him* there is no darkness.

A Prayer from Denise:

Father God, I thank You for this time together in Your Word, and for seeing these amazing holy truths. Lord, these truths can be like mysteries because they can be so hard for us to understand — but we believe. We take You at Your Word, Lord — Your Word is truth: Your Holy Spirit came into us, eradicated the darkness in our lost spirit, and brought Your light to illuminate our spirit with Your presence. Someday we're going to see You lighting up Heaven, for You ARE Light, and we will be with You forever and ever and ever. We give You praise and glory, and we thank You for Your mighty presence. In Jesus' name. Amen.

STUDY QUESTIONS

Study to shew thyself approved unto God, a workman that needeth not to be ashamed, rightly dividing the word of truth.
— 2 Timothy 2:15

1. Read Genesis 1:1-5. What is the very first thing that God spoke into existence? How does knowing this truth impact your understanding of His presence in your life and what He does once His Spirit comes to live inside you?

2. In Jesus' conversation with Pilate and His response to the accusations of the crowd in John 18:28-38, what did He say about Himself — and about *you* — in verse 37? (*See also* John 10:27,28.)

PRACTICAL APPLICATION

> But be ye doers of the word, and not hearers only,
> deceiving your own selves.
> —James 1:22

1. Did you realize before this lesson that you truly cannot escape the presence of the Father, Jesus, and the Holy Spirit? Has there ever been a time when you thought God was absent from you? Why did you think so? How does it change your perspective to know that He is with you now and always has been?

2. Can you remember a time or place where it felt nearly impossible to see clearly? Is there any area of life where you currently feel that way? Take a moment to ask the Holy Spirit to shine His light on you and your situation and watch for Him to make your path straight.

LESSON 4

TOPIC

God Has a Wonderful Book About You

SCRIPTURES

1. **Psalm 139:11** (*NASB*) — If I say, "Surely the darkness will overwhelm me...."

2. **Psalm 139:11** (*AMP*) — "...The night will be the only light around me."

3. **John 1:5** — And the light shines in the darkness, and the darkness did not comprehend it.

4. **Psalm 139:13,14** — For You formed my inward parts; You covered me in my mother's womb. I will praise You, for I am fearfully and wonderfully made....

5. **Psalm 139:15-18** — My frame was not hidden from You, when I was made in secret, and skillfully wrought in the lowest parts of the earth. Your eyes saw my substance, being yet unformed. And in Your book they all were written...How precious also are Your thoughts to me, O God! How great is the sum of them! If I should count them, they would be more in number than the sand; when I awake, I am still with You.

SYNOPSIS

God is so attentive to His children that He actually has an entire book about each of us that contains every single detail of every single day of our lives. He sees us as His priceless treasures; we are His works of art that reflect His image and personality. Our body is incredibly complex, valuable, and wonderfully designed to keep us alive and running well, and it was knit together by God Himself. Our heart and soul were intentionally created by Him to fulfill a precious, needed purpose unique to each and every one of us.

The emphasis of this lesson:

God's knowledge of you has been complete since before you were born. He knit you together beautifully, body and soul, for an amazing destiny and friendship with Him, and He's constantly thinking loving thoughts toward you.

This study on *How Good Is God?* has been all about the immense love of God, which is so important for us to fully grasp. In fact, Paul said in Ephesians 3:18, that he hopes all believers will know "the width and length the depth and height" of God's love, which David so beautifully expressed in Psalm 139. David continued his psalm to the Lord in verse 11: "If I say, 'Surely the darkness will overwhelm me...' (*NASB*), '...The night will be the only light around me...'" (*AMP*).

The power of light *always* extinguishes the power of darkness. In the same way, love overcomes and displaces hate, because love is more powerful than hate. Think about it: Jesus loved us so much that He took on all of our hate, shame, guilt, sin, sickness, and poverty. He took on all that darkness, and He shattered that darkness with His love. *Hallelujah!*

The apostle John also had a revelation of God's love. In John 1:5, he said:

And the light shines in the darkness, and the darkness did not comprehend it.

In the *New International Version*, the second part of the verse reads, "...And the darkness has not overcome it." Again we see that the darkness has never — and never will — overcome the Light, which is Jesus. He has been the Light forever, since before we were even thought of or born. In Psalm 139:13 and 14, David said,

For You formed my inward parts; You covered me in my mother's womb.

When David said, "You formed my inward parts," he was poetically telling the Lord, "You wove them together." Inside your mother's womb, God in His power was weaving every fiber of you together. Isn't that amazing? He was painstakingly, intentionally fashioning and creating you with every day of your life on earth in mind. In verse 14, David responded to this revelation:

I will praise You, for I am fearfully and wonderfully made....

Isn't that beautiful? You've probably heard this verse quoted countless times, and it's a wonderful and absolutely true thing to say over your body. Go ahead and confess right now, "I am fearfully and wonderfully made." And you're about to see how *very* fearfully and how *very* wonderfully you truly are made.

What Earth Calls Cheap, God Calls Priceless

If we were to "melt" or "break down" the human body to carbon, coal, calcium, or sugar — all the minerals of which our body is composed — some biblical commentators say it would be worth from .98 cents to $5.00. Not very much, right? Well, what God is doing with that which has seemingly very little value is truly incredible.

Did you know that in the human body, there are 206 bones, 600 muscles, and *ten thousands* of miles of blood vessels? Can you imagine that?

Here are a few more facts about the human body that will astound you:

- There are between 16,000-20,000 hair cells in your ears that organize and communicate sound to your brain so you can hear.[1]
- One square inch of your skin contains 95-100 oil glands, 9.5 million cells, and 650 sweat glands.[2]
- There are 600 million air cells in your lungs that inhale 2,400 gallons of air to keep you alive every single day.[3]
- Your heart beats an incredible 4,200 times every hour and on average pumps 2,000 gallons of blood daily.[4]

Who can do that? Only God! And He did all this with something that people say is only worth $1-$5. Your body is a truly miraculous, beautifully designed gift from your Creator. Psalm 14:1 affirms that *a fool* says in his heart, "There is no God." But we are *not* fools — *praise God!*

Can you imagine looking at the incredible complexities of the human body, and thinking, *This was a complete accident; a fluke of nature — there's no God?*

Friend, there is a God who is alive, loves you, and put you together so intentionally and beautifully that you don't even have to think about telling your heart to beat or your lungs to breathe. In Psalm 139:15, David continued writing about his awe and wonder of God. He wrote:

My frame was not hidden from You, when I was made in secret, and skillfully wrought in the lowest parts of the earth.

When David mentioned his "frame," he was elaborating on how God masterfully and completely uniquely created even our bone structure; each person's skeletal system is specific to that person. Your veins, your nerves, your skin — every part of you from your conception — was embroidered by God inside your mother's womb.

Before We Had Even Lived One Day, God Knew All Our Days

God skillfully and intricately weaves the human body together throughout the whole growth process. In Psalm 139:16, David mentioned how God oversaw the entire process of his development from the time he was in his mother's womb. He said,

Your eyes saw my substance, being yet unformed. And in Your book they all were written, the days fashioned for me, when as yet there were none of them.

As David was writing this, he clearly had a revelation of how God sees our whole life at one time, even from the embryo stage of growth before the organs have developed and the body can live independently. God's eyes were on you at conception. From that first moment, He saw you developing and had every day of your life written in a book — before you had lived even one of them. Somewhere in Heaven, there are books of people's lives, and one of these books has *your* name on it and it is filled with every single detail of your life. Isn't that amazing?

Imagine for a minute a very expensive car — maybe one like a Mercedes-Benz. This vehicle is an incredibly detailed and complex creation. Do you really think that every single part and how it was put together is *not* written down somewhere? Of course, it is. Every detail about it is documented. And that's only a car! How much more important would it be to God to record all the details of *you* — your creation, development, birth, and entire life — in one of His books? You are His masterpiece (*see* Ephesians 2:10)!

You truly are wonderfully made *on* purpose and *for* a purpose. As God was making you, He thought intentionally about the shape of your nose, the color of your eyes and the distance between them, the texture of your hair, your height, and all the proportions of your body, and He wrote it all down. That's how absolutely precious you are to Him.

The word "fashioned" in Psalm 139:16 refers to the days which God has *ordained* for your creation. As God was weaving you together, He knew exactly how you would be fashioned and everything about your life. He purposely had planned out how He would make you. He was deliberate and intentional — you are NOT a mistake!

You might be thinking, *This is just too much. How in the world can this be true?* David had the exact same thought, and he expressed it in verses 17 and 18. David pondered,

How precious also are Your thoughts to me, O God! How great is the sum of them! If I should count them, they would be more in number than the sand; when I awake, I am still with You.

David was overwhelmed by what he was understanding and realizing about the love of God. The fact that God loved him before he was even formed in his mother's womb and that every single fact about him had been recorded by God long before he'd had even one conscious thought was weighty knowledge. And even more, God's thoughts about him — and about each of us — can never run out. These thoughts outnumber the grains of sand on all the beaches of the world. And all this is true from the very beginning of your life!

It is such a sacred, eternal, and important time when God is creating someone in the womb — that's one of many reasons why abortion is so wrong. It is both murder and stealing the life of a child — a person that was delicately, tenderly, and lovingly formed by God Himself. It is preventing this unique creation from ever taking his or her first breath, and robbing the world of the gift that they will be.

[**Note:** If you are reading this and you've had an abortion, know that God loves you so much and absolutely has grace and forgiveness for you. There's *no* condemnation for those who are in Christ (*see* Romans 8:1). First John 1:9 says that when we confess our sin, He is faithful to forgive us and cleanse us from *all* unrighteousness. So know that you are forgiven, free, and perfectly loved by the same God who intentionally created and designed you in *your* mother's womb.]

Reflecting on Psalm 139:17, David basically said, "Even if I busy myself all night trying to count Your thoughts about me, when I wake up, they're still there. They are innumerable! I just lay here and think about how amazing it is that You created me, God. You saw my substance and You knit me together, Lord. It's so amazing, and You've even written everything about me in a book. You love me so much! God, You are so incredible."

In the same way, God's love and thoughts towards *you* are immeasurable, constant, and forever. I pray you know more and more with each passing day how wide and long, how high and deep is His love for you!

A Prayer from Denise:

I thank You, God, for Your power, Your unconditional love, and Your eyes that were upon me when You were creating me in my mother's womb. Thank You for creating me so uniquely and beautifully. Give me grace to grow in my understanding of who You are, how much You love me, and the specific plans You have for my life. I love you, Father. You are a mighty God, and I give You all the praise, glory, and honor. In Jesus' name. Amen.

STUDY QUESTIONS

Study to shew thyself approved unto God, a workman that needeth not to be ashamed, rightly dividing the word of truth.
— 2 Timothy 2:15

1. God's thoughts about you are countless — completely innumerable — and He never leaves you alone to fend for yourself. What else does the Bible say about God's thoughts? (*See* Zephaniah 3:17, Jeremiah 29:11, and Isaiah 55:9.)

2. God knew exactly how He wanted to design you, and He created you personally and intimately in your mother's womb for an amazing purpose that only you can fulfill. Who is mentioned in the Bible as having a specific direction and destiny, even before they were born? (*Hint*: Read Jeremiah 1:5 and Judges 13.)

PRACTICAL APPLICATION

But be ye doers of the word, and not hearers only, deceiving your own selves.
— James 1:22

1. Were you surprised to learn about the book that God has written about your life? What else does He have in Heaven with your name on it (*see* Psalm 56:8)?

2. What tears have you cried while waiting for God to bring an answer to your pain? Take a moment to thank Him for His comfort in the middle of whatever wounds remain in your heart.

3. You — yes, *you* — are fearfully and wonderfully made. Your body, soul, and spirit are perfectly crafted for the plans and purposes God has set apart for you. What is one thing about yourself that you've struggled to love? Whether it's a physical trait, personality trait, or something else, bring that up to Him. Ask Him to show you how He sees that trait in you and how He sees *you* — His precious son or daughter — and then listen. Write down what He says, so you can hold on to and reflect on *His* loving perspective of you when you need it most.

[1] Joyce Dall 'Acqua Peterson, "Tuning in to the inner ear," The Jackson Laboratory, May 21, 2018, https://www.jax.org/news-and-insights/2018/May/tuning-in -to-the-inner-ear.

[2] Patty Young, M.D., https://www.premierplasticsurgeryoftexas.com/skin-care -procedures-plano/body/skin-facts.

[3] National Geographic writers, "Lungs," National Geographic.com, https://www.nationalgeographic.com/science/article/lungs.

[4] Phoenix Heart, "3 Things Most Don't Know About Their Heart," https://www.phoenixheart.com/blog/3-things-most-dont-know-about-their-heart.

Notes

CLAIM YOUR FREE RESOURCE!

As a way of introducing you further to the teaching ministry of Rick Renner, we would like to send you FREE of charge his teaching, "How To Receive a Miraculous Touch From God" on CD or USB format.

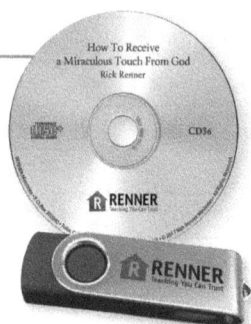

In His earthly ministry, Jesus commonly healed *all* who were sick of *all* their diseases. In this profound message, learn about the manifold dimensions of Christ's wisdom, goodness, power, and love toward all humanity who came to Him in faith with their needs.

☑ **YES, I want to receive Rick Renner's monthly teaching letter!**

Simply scan the QR code to claim this resource or go to: **renner.org/claim-your-free-offer**

www.ingramcontent.com/pod-product-compliance
Lightning Source LLC
Chambersburg PA
CBHW070756050426
42452CB00010B/1867